Smoothie Recipe Book To Gain Energy & Detox 17 Smoothie Bowl Recipes, Cleanse Drinks & Blender Mix Recipes To Feel Stronger

Juliana Baltimoore

Published by InfinitYou, 2017.

While every precaution has been taken in the preparation of this book, the publisher assumes no responsibility for errors or omissions, or for damages resulting from the use of the information contained herein.

SMOOTHIE RECIPE BOOK TO GAIN ENERGY & DETOX 17 SMOOTHIE BOWL RECIPES, CLEANSE DRINKS & BLENDER MIX RECIPES TO FEEL STRONGER

First edition. July 12, 2017.

Copyright © 2017 Juliana Baltimoore.

ISBN: 978-1386016731

Written by Juliana Baltimoore.

Nutribullet Quiz

O	D	E	U	J	B	Y	H	M	U	L	S	D	Y	F
R	G	I	N	G	E	R	H	N	B	O	C	W	Q	S
H	T	R	H	Y	X	T	Y	B	A	I	Y	Q	T	E
I	E	A	N	U	T	R	I	B	U	L	L	E	T	C
M	O	G	H	C	I	N	N	A	M	O	N	E	A	U
A	Q	P	Q	B	A	O	L	A	R	U	P	U	U	L
O	H	J	N	G	R	E	E	N	S	M	N	Y	F	L
B	E	R	R	I	E	S	J	A	V	O	C	A	D	O
X	H	E	R	B	F	B	E	E	T	R	O	O	T	U
J	X	J	P	X	X	I	O	N	Y	S	W	M	F	I
V	O	B	L	E	N	D	E	R	X	I	P	I	H	R
B	A	N	A	N	A	E	B	W	H	I	G	L	T	V
E	T	T	T	L	E	U	V	I	T	A	M	I	X	D
Y	D	S	P	I	N	A	C	H	P	U	L	U	F	A
W	X	K	A	R	C	Y	U	E	E	T	L	A	R	N

Nutribullet Quiz

The Powerful 5 Minute Smoothie Ritual

- 1 Package of frozen spinach
- 1 Cup of organic non fat Italian ricotta cheese
- 1 Fresh organic egg
- 1/4 Cup of shredded mozzarella
- 4 Lasagna noodles
- 2 Cups really good self made pasta sauce
- Turkey, chicken or other type of meat
- A dash of pink Himalaya salt

- 1 Tablespoon of organic pumpkin seeds
- 1 Tablespoon of organic sunflower seeds
- 1 Organic small apple, without seeds and sliced into quarters
- 1 Small organic carrot
- 1 Small ripe banana
- 1 Cup of fresh organic blueberries
- 1 Cup of fresh organic baby spinach and kale spinach)
- 4-5 Pieces of organic asparagus if possible
- 1 Cup of fresh organic raspberries
- 1 Tablespoon of flax meal
- 1 Cup of vanilla soy milk
- 1 Cup of organic coconut water

- Some of your favorite greens
- 1 Banana
- 1 Cup of grapes
- 1 Pear
- Few walnuts
- Fresh sping water

2 Leaves of lettuce
1 Pear
1 Apple
1 Cup of blueberries
1 Banana
1 Teaspoon of maca powder
Some fresh spring water

Hand full of spinach
1/2 Avocado
1 Cup of unsweetened yoghurt
1 Tablespoon of Hemp seeds
1 Scoop of almond butter
Cinnamon ground
1 Cup of almond milk
3 Ice cubes

1 Hand full of spinach
1 Cup of blueberries
1/2 Cup of seedless black grapes
Almonds
Cup almond milk unsweetened
1 Scoop of protein powder
1 Cup of sugar cane juice

1/2 Avocado
1 Small cucumber
2 Small sized carrots
1 Beetroot
Cup of wheat grass

1 Pineapple
1 Bunch of spinach
1 Banana
1/2 Cup of wheat grass
1 Apple
1 Cup of water

2 Hands full of fresh hebs

1 Hand full of postelein herbs

1 Hand full of Asian salad

2 small sweet Apples

1 Small ripe banana

1/2 Lemon

1 Piece of fresh ginger

1-2 Teaspoon of Himalaya

Fresh sping water

1 Portion of frozen mixed berries

Unsweetened almond milk

Half of a banana

1 Scoop of protein powder

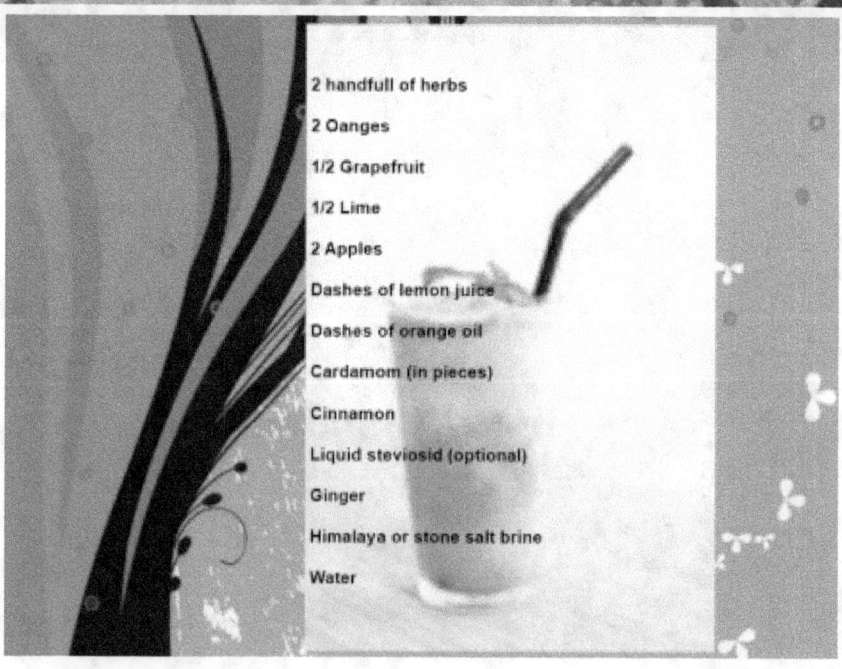

2 handfull of herbs

2 Oanges

1/2 Grapefruit

1/2 Lime

2 Apples

Dashes of lemon juice

Dashes of orange oil

Cardamom (in pieces)

Cinnamon

Liquid steviosid (optional)

Ginger

Himalaya or stone salt brine

Water

1 Can of drained chickpeas

1 Clove of garlic

1 handful of fresh spinach

Steamed or marinated artichoke hearts

1 Lemon

Some pita chips and chickpeas

Introduction

People all around the globe are increasingly feeding on manufactured and unhealthy food items. However, ardent food lovers like myself have turned to high speed blender recipes (in my case Nutribullet recipes) for the most delicious, clean, lean and nutritious recipes that are specifically meant to boost a healthy living free from calories, fats, and other unhealthy ingredients.

Our health is the most important thing and we are always told take care of your body and it will take care of us when we are old.

Modern lifestyle makes it very hard to live a clean, healthy and balanced lifestyle with food that is good for our body and brain.

We are all faced by numerous health challenges related to food, this is why I have researched the best clean eating and clean drinking high speed blender recipes that are not only supplying the body with healthy nutrients and ingredients, but I also made sure that they are tasty and delicious at the same time.

The Nutribullet has become my favorite kitchen supply because these Nutribullet recipes that I have turned into this compilation of Nutribullet recipes are helping me and my family enhance our health and clean eating and drinking lifestyle on a daily basis. The Nutribullet is surprisingly effective. Try adding these and other ingredients for a flavorful experience: ground oatmeal, peanut butter, yogurt, applesauce, cocoa powder, fruit juice and cinnamon.

The Nutribullet is very flexible and multifunctional and I am using it on a daily basis to make tasty:

Nutrition/Protein Shakes
Healthy Smoothies
Yogurt Smoothies
Nutritious Drinks
Scrambled Eggs
Egg Batter for Omelets & Egg Dishes
Pies & Cakes
Pancake Batter
French-Toast Batter
Meal Replacement Drinks
Pasta Sauces
Dips
Relishes
Chutneys
Yoghurts, Desserts & Puddings
Salad Dressing Mixes
Lump-Free Gravy

I am sure that there are many other applications and usages for other food and drink preparations, but today let's focus on the the clean, lean and healthy high-speed blender (in my case Nutribullet recipes) that are proven and tested by myself, my family and friends.

We all love these high-speed blender recipes so much because not only are they healthy and delicious, but they are a true time saver, too. Since I am an on-line marketer and always on the go, I do understand the importance of having a convenient healthy snacks around.

When I first began with my online business I was struggling to maintain my weight.

This was due to all the high fat and sugar foods that I was eating.

During this time I built up a lot of toxins in my body and began to get sick plus I have been suffering from Asthma and breathing problems for a long time.

After talking to my sister she told me about these healthy, clean and lean Nutribullet smoothies, drinks and other delicious dishes she is making with the help of her Nutribullet high-speed blender.

These recipes work really great and can be made quickly. This is the perfect lifestyle solution for me as I need a healthy snack during my many work hours on the computer.

I have included my 17 most amazing high-speed blender (in my case Nutribullet recipes) that have been most effective in achieving my goal to live a lifestyle with clean eating & drinking, to beat my health problems and to achieve a lean body as a result from these recipes in combination with a light yoga and meditation routine. In my case the Nutribullet is my favorite high-speed blender, but you can use your own favorite high-speed blender or regular blender that you have at home.

These recipes are all healthy and delicious at the same time so that you can start replacing your common and unhealthy food items and ingredients that are making you sick or gain weight with these clean food and drink ingredients.

If time and a healthy lifestyle are a concern, you will love these effortless 5 minute easy to make high-speed blender recipes that keep you healthy, lean and clean!

I hope you'll enjoy these recipes like my friends and family enjoy them every day!

My Favorite Quote

All I know is it took me 5 minutes to get it running – Juliana Baldacini

The Proper Blender & Preparation

What is the proper blender?

Not every beginner has the perfect Turbomixer like the Nutribullet or the Vitamix available. Don't worry if you don't have it yet.

You can also use a common kitchen blender or mixer until it stops working and then you can invest in your dream machine.

Top blenders are brands like the Nutribullet, Vitamix, Revoblend, etc.

However, the Nutribullet is a high speed power blender that is able to give the best of both worlds. It is a blender and a juicer all at the same time.

The inventor of the Nutribullet blender calls it the Extractor.

Why?

Simply because the Nutribullet is so powerful and it does the same job like a juicer does only to keep the pulp of the fruits in the drink.

As I told you in the introduction, my sister Alecandra recommended it to me and I bought it immediately. I have experimented and done many amazing blender and juicing jobs with it and do not want to miss it one day because I actually use it every day.

The Nutribullet makes any type of smoothie, juice or mixture of liquid consistency in mere seconds.

The part that I like the best is that it takes not even one minute to clean it and enjoy another amazing Nutribullet recipe.

I have about three other regular blenders at home. Since my Nutribullet arrived at my front door, I hardly use my old blender anymore because they are old school and I do not like the long cleaning process.

They just lack the power to do the job and to taste like the recipes that I am able to make with my Nutribullet.

If you are mainly preparing only cold ingredients, I even prefer the Nutribullet to the Vitamix 1782 TurboBlend, 2 Speed.

The Vitamix is able to also blend hot ingredients like soups and sauces, but if you are following for example my Spaghetti Nutribullet recipe, I will show you how you can use your microwave in combination with the Nutribullet and like this you are not only saving a lot of money, but also a lot of cleaning time because the Vitamix is much more expensive and bigger so the cleaning process is longer, too.

In terms of power the Nutribullet almost beats the Vitamix because it gives you more flexibility and it is just a blender that is in my opinion more powerful and more compatible to our modern and mobile lifestyle needs.

Why I love my Nutribullet high-speed blender most:

I clean up after each recipe in a snap and the cleaning process is a breeze. I can try go into my kitchen and make one of my clean eating or drinking recipes, clean up and be out of there in 5 minutes.

I love that my clean smoothie recipes come out not complete liquid but really well blended and the texture and consistency is perfect.

The nutrition stays inside and I can keep the nutrition of the pulp which is the most beneficial for the body.

At the beginning I had some leaking issues, but this is not a major thing because when I reduced the content under the Max Fill Line on the container, I solved that issue ASAP!

Tearing even through kale, chard, frozen berries, almonds, chia seeds, coconut, walnuts, Brazilian nuts, and other hard ingredients has never been easier.

I just love the high-power speed of it, the flexibility and the fact that I can juice and do smoothies at the same time, the light weight so I can even take it with me when I am on the go. I am a very mobile person and do travel a lot and this is the only kitchen supply that I would take with me on a longer trip. This is why the Nutribullet is part of my lifestyle technology.

Preparation:

The basic preparation for each Nutribullet recipe is to simply add all the ingredients into a Nutribullet mixer or other high-speed blender like a Vitamix or similar blender.

For the Smoothie recipes you can add some fresh spring water, if needed in order to reach your desired thickness.

Use organic products for all the recipes if possible.

Quantities for the Recipes:

I will not make specific quantities in (milli) grams or (Milli) liters or ounces just because you need to learn to trust your own preferences.

Smoothies for example are not only easy to prepare, they are super easy to prepare. In this sense, my recipes are primarily there to show you the ingredients and give you lots of inspiration!

Therefore, it is my motto to get you inspired and encourage you to experiment a little bit with the ingredients and adjusts the individual recipes to your own preferences!

This is especially true for all the smoothie recipes!

Amazing Nutribullet Recipe: Pita Chips Sauce

I must confess that I am a huge fan of this tasty Nutribullet recipe for Pita Chips Sauce.

The recipe is simple to follow and easier to make than ever before meaning no time is wasted in the kitchen while preparing the delicacy.

I also love this particular recipe since it gives an option of using pepper at the very end, and being a chilli person, this is mouth-watering enough for me.

Ingredients:
1 can of drained chickpeas
1 clove of garlic
1 handful of fresh spinach
steamed or marinated artichoke hearts depending on your preference
a whole lemon for the lemon juice
some pita chips and chickpeas

5 Minute Quick Nutribullet Preparation:

To prepare the pita chips sauce, you will require a can of drained chickpeas where about a quarter is saved for the liquid, a clove of garlic, a handful of fresh spinach, steamed or marinated artichoke hearts depending on your preference, a whole lemon for the lemon juice and some pita chips and chickpeas.

Mix all the ingredients thoroughly except for the pita chips to attain a nice blend of the items stated.

It is in this blend that you will add salt to your own taste. For the pepper-heads like me, add pepper to your desired taste.

This is then served with some salty pita chips to provide a simple yet amazing snack or appetizer that is not only healthy and nutritious, but it tastes awesome and you will get all the compliments.

I have tried out all kinds of blenders before, but my family loves the Pita Chips Sauce that is made with the Nutribullet blender most. The Nutribullet just produces the best texture and I have not been able to make it creamier with any other blender.

Amazing Nutribullet Recipe 2: Spaghetti Sauce Recipe

My husband is Italian and that is why I have included two amazing Nutribullet recipes that he approves of because of the taste.

I don't know how much you know about old traditional Italian families, but everything revolves around food. According to him and his family, a good spaghetti dinner will bring the family together and it makes everyone happy and cheerful.

Since I make this Spaghetti dish with my new Nutribullet blender, he encourages me to make it more often because he really loves what the high power of a Nutriblender can even add in terms of flavor and taste to his favorite dish!

Ingredients:
8 ounces of Italian spaghetti noodles
1/4 cup of homemade chicken broth

10 -15 organic cherry tomatoes (you can replace them with a regular tomato, slice and quarter it)

1 white organic pearl onion (you can replace it with 1/4 cup of a chopped and regular onion)

2 tablespoons of Italian red wine (you can replace the wine with chicken broth or more water if you like)

2 tablespoons of organic tomatoe paste

2 organic garlic cloves

2 springs of organic basil

1/4 cup of ground beef (you can replace the beef with turkey)

1 pinch of original Italian seasoning (totally optional)

organic salt and pepper and to your liking

10 Minute Quick Nutribullet Preparation - Cooking time: 10 Minutes:

First start boiling salted water to cook the spaghetti. Follow the packages direction for the cooking process.

Add all the spaghetti sauce ingredients into the tall cup of your Nutribullet and twist on the crossblade.

Next, place the cup on your NutriBullet blender and press it down on the cup for one second and then release the pressure.

Pause and let the ingredients settle.

Quickly pulse again.

Repeat the pulsing procedure and until the ingredients have a good looking consistency

Next, go ahead and twist off the crossblade and next twist on the large holed Shaker-Steamer top.

Go ahead and place the cup in a microwave and cook on high level for around 9 to 10 minutes and until the meat is well cooked.

All microwaves vary so check regularly.

If the meat looks dry remove the cup and stir the mixture and also add some more red wine, water or broth.

Return it to the microwave and finish the cooking process.

Serve your hot Spaghetti sauce over the hot and steamy pasta. Garnish with a basil leave and some grated Italian parmesan cheese.

Serve the dish with a chilled Italian white or red wine and enjoy:)

Tip:

Make sure to save some of this delicious Spaghetti sauce for the Healthy yummie Ricotta Dinner that is also included in this book.

Amazing Nutribullet Recipe 3: Citrus Fruit Power Smoothie

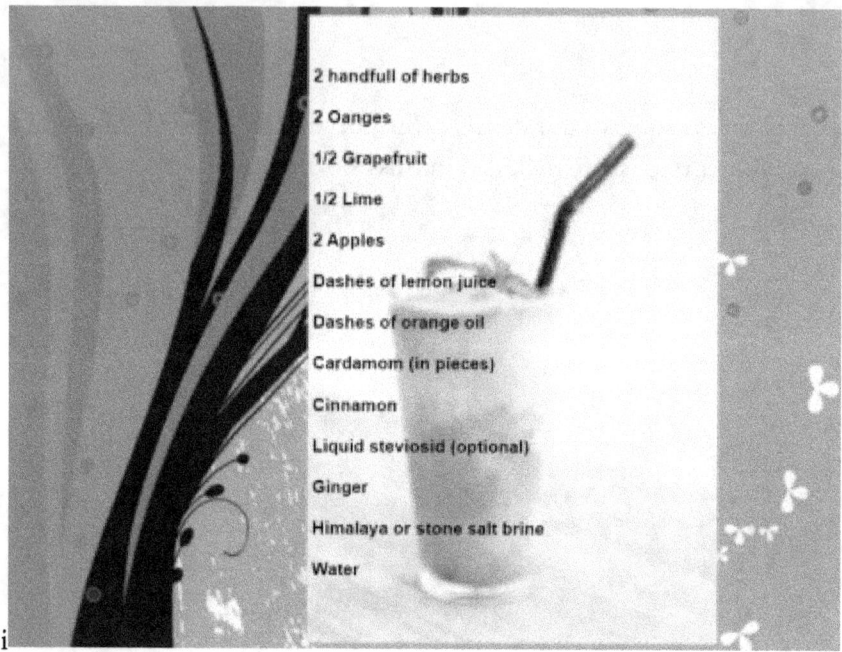

This Citrus Fruit Power Smoothie tastes fantastic. It is a perfect Smoothie for the summer time because it is very refreshing. The smart combination of the citrus fruits makes this smoothie a winner. The spices are a nice add on. The orange oil gives the final touch!

Ingredients:

2 handfull of wild hebs (nettle, dandelion, plantain, young linden and birch leaves)
2 small juice oranges (organic if possible)
1/2 half of a grapefruit including some rind! (organic if possible)
1/2 of a lime (with no rind and organic if possible)
2 small apples (brand: Braeburn)
some dashes of lemon juice
some dashes of orange oil (optional)
1 pinch of cardamom (in pieces)
1 pinch of cinnamon

1- 2 drops of liquid steviosid (optional)
1 piece of ginger
2 teaspoon of Himalaya or stone salt brine
water to your liking

5 Minute Nutribullet Preparation:

Simply add all the ingredients into a Nutribullet mixer or other high-speed blender like a Vitamix or similar blender. Add water, if needed in order to reach your desired thickness.

Amazing Nutribullet Recipe 4: Berry Breakfast Smoothie

Another beverage I recommend especially for breakfast is the Berry Breakfast Smoothie.

Ingredients:
1 portion of frozen mixed berries
unsweetened almond milk
half of a banana
1 scoop of protein powder

5 Minute Quick Nutribullet Preparation:
You are encouraged to use your favorite protein powder.
Make a concoction of the ingredients by blending them together continuously for 15-20 seconds.

Then serve this delicious Nutribullet Berry Breakfast Smoothie for the ultimate enjoyment.

I am into this perfect berry breakfast protein smoothie as it helps start the day with the vitality and vigor needed for our day-to-day activities.

I also use it on most of the mornings to surprise my loved ones who usually drain their glasses in sheer enjoyment.

This is a very healthy way to start your day and the Nutribullet blender is helping you make this nutritious Smoothie in a quick 5 minute way.

Amazing Nutribullet Recipe 5: Strawberry Milk Shake

- 3 Frozen strawberries
- 1 Teaspoonful of cacao powder
- 11/2 Cups of unsweetened almond milk
- 1 Teaspoonful of chia powder

Moving on, the strawberry milkshake is also one of my must-have Nutribullet recipes.

The beverage leaves a lovely taste on the mouth and it is no surprise that I find myself making it repeatedly given the ease of preparation.

I love this shake as it is low in fats, carbs, and calories hence a very healthy option for a beverage.

Ingredients:

3 frozen strawberries

1 teaspoonful of cacao powder

1 1/2 cups of unsweetened almond milk

1 teaspoonful of chia powder

5 Minute Quick Nutribullet Preparation:

The simple instructions of making this delicious Nutribullet Strawberry Milkshake are just by blending the ingredients completely in your Nutribullet blender for around 20 seconds.

The drink is therefore ready for you to enjoy, but my advice is to chill it in the fridge for a while to give it a cooling effect.

Like this you will enjoy every single sip that you are going to take.

Amazing Nutribullet Recipe 6: Banana Berry Power Smoothie

The Banana Berry Power Smoothie tastes like more. Everybody who tried it could not resist and it is my tested and proven one. The secret of this recipe is the combination of banana and blueberry. Enjoy this delicious and healthy Nutribullet smoothie recipe.

Ingredients:
1 hand full of dandelion
1 hand full of parsley
2 small and ripe bananas
2 hand full of blueberries
The juice of half of a lemon
1-2 teaspoon of Himalaya or stone salt brine
Fresh spring water to your liking

5 Minute Nutribullet Preparation:

Simply add all the ingredients into a Nutribullet mixer or other high-speed blender like a Vitamix or similar blender. Add water, if needed in order to reach your desired thickness.

Amazing Nutribullet Recipe 7: Fruity Furnace Fat-Burning Nutriblast

2 Hands full of fresh hebs

1 Hand full of postelein herbs

1 Hand full of Asian salad

2 small sweet Apples

1 Small ripe banana

1/2 Lemon

1 Piece of fresh ginger

1-2 Teaspoon of Himalaya

Fresh sping water

This smoothie is full of wild herbs like nettle, ground elder, dandelions and plantain.

By the way hot stands for the fact that this Nutribullet recipe makes use of the Asian salad which relates to the spicy radish.

Ingredients:

2 hands full of fresh herbs (Nettle, dandelion, ground elder)
　1 hand full of postelein herbs
　1 hand full of Asian salad (or another seasonal salad that you like)
　2 small sweet Apples (brand: Red Prince if possible)
　1 small ripe banana
　1/2 lemon
　1 piece of fresh ginger
　1-2 teaspoon of Himalaya or stone salt brine
　Fresh spring water to your liking

5 Minute Quick Nutribullet Preparation:

With the help of a Nutribullet blender simply add all the above ingredients into your Nutribullet.

Turn it on your machine and watch as everything combines into a smoothie texture.

Pour this healthy tasty treat into your favorite glass and enjoy a sip or place it in the fridge for later use.

Amazing Nutribullet Recipe 8: Toxic Blaster

1 Pineapple
1 Bunch of spinach
1 Banana
1/2 Cup of wheat grass
1 Apple
1 Cup of water

The Toxic Blaster is a true fat burner. If you are also looking to lose some weight and become lean and clean at the same time, this fat burning Nutribullet recipe is called the Toxic Blaster.

The Toxic Blaster also helps you to wash out all the toxins in your body and make you healthy by cleaning your blood.

Ingredients:

¼ pineapple (medium size)
a bunch of organic spinach
1 small ripe banana
1/2 cup of wheat grass
1 small apple
1 cup of fresh spring water

5 Minute Quick Nutribullet Preparation: (In fact the preparation only takes you 3 times for preparation and 1 minute for blending it)

Clean the pineapple, spinach then chop the banana and pineapple to cubes.

Next, take all the ingredients and mix them in a Nutriblast blender and blend the ingredients.

The Toxic Blaster is best when you are drinking it in the morning before doing anything else. Later you can eat some light breakfast, but you will have the best effect with cleaning out all the toxins if you have the Toxic Blaster first thing in the morning.

Amazing Nutribullet Recipe 9: Nutri Blaster

This nutritious superfood Nutribullet recipe is called the Nutri-Drink. It is one of my all-time favorite especially when I am feeling like my body is weak and I am about to get sick.

Here is what you need for this awesome Nutribullet recipe.

Ingredients:

1/2 avocado (medium)
1 small sized cucumber (organic if possible)
2 small sized carrots (organic if possible)
1 beetroot (organic if possible)
½ cup of wheat grass

5 Minute Quick Nutribullet Preparation:

Clean the cucumber, carrots, beetroot and the avocado.
Peel the carrots and the avocado.
Chop the carrot cucumber and beet root into medium sized cubes.
Mix all the ingredients in your Nutribullet blender and blend for 1 minute or until all the ingredient are well blended together and you like the texture.

This recipe is very tasty, nutritious and healthy at the same time. It improves and boosts your immune system.

Amazing Nutribullet Recipe 10: Purple Smoothie

The Purple smoothie has a very nice purple color to it and can be taken whenever you need some extra energy during the day.

Ingredients:
1 hand full of spinach (organic if possible)
½ cup of blueberries (organic if possible)
1/2 cup of seedless black grapes (organic if possible)
½ almonds
¼ cup almond milk unsweetened
1 scoop of protein powder
½ cup of sugar cane juice

5 Minute Quick Nutribullet Preparation:
Clean the spinach, blueberries, and black grapes until they are clean.

Mix all the ingredients in a Nutribullet blender for 30 seconds to 1 minute until all the ingredients are well blended.

The purple smoothie is a good breakfast replacement, especially if you are trying to lose some weight.

If you are following a healthy food lifestyle, I recommend the Purple smoothie any day because it energizes the body and you can start your day stress free because this Nutribullet recipe gives your body all the health benefits and nutrients that it needs in order to function in a relaxed and balanced way.

Amazing Nutribullet Recipe 11: Fungal Free Smoothie

The Fungal Free Smoothie is very good for women since it helps to prevent and also treat fungal bacteria in the body like candida that women sometimes suffer from.

Ingredients:
A hand full of spinach (organic if possible)
1/2 small avocado (organic if possible)
1 cup of unsweetened yoghurt
1 tablespoon of hemp seeds
1 scoop of almond butter
½ tbsp. cinnamon ground
1 cup of almond milk unsweetened (optional)
3 ice cubes
5 Minute Quick Nutribullet Preparation:

Clean the spinach and avocado well then mix all the ingredients in the Nutribullet blender until all the ingredients have been well blended.

This recipe also has fat but not the bad fat that can add weight. This recipe contains the good fat that helps the body and keeps your body lean and clean.

Amazing Nutribullet Recipe 12: Nature's Candy

This is the Natural Candy that makes you feel dandy! You willl definitely feel better after drinking the Nature's Candy recipe as the ingredients come together to balance and regulate the hormones of your body.

Ingredients:
    2 leaves of lettuce (organic if possible)
    1 pear (organic if possible)
    1 apple (organic if possible)
    1 cup of blueberries (organic if possible)
    1 banana (organic if possible)
    1 teaspoon of maca powder
    Some fresh spring water to your liking

5 Minute Quick Nutribullet Preparation:

After mixing the water and maca powder together, simply pour the items into the Nutribullet and puree them.

After it is mixed to your liking the drink can be poured into glasses or placed in the fridge for later use.

Tips:

Each day I will use one of these wonderful recipes as a meal replacement for breakfast, lunch or dinner. The best part about using these different drinks is they actually work!

I love these Nutribullet smoothie and drink recipes because they helps me keep healthy as well as satisfied.

Also, all of the ingredients that are needed to make these recipes can be found at your local market for less than $9!

Amazing Nutribullet Recipe 13: Energy Elixir

This energizing treat will move your feet and you will need the following ingredients.

Ingredients:
some of your favorite greens (organic if possible)
1 banana (organic if possible)
1 cup of grapes (organic if possible)
1 pear (organic if possible)
few walnuts
fresh spring water to your liking

5 Minute Quick Nutribullet Preparation:

Pour all of the ingredients into your Nutribullet and add the water. Turn on your machine and let the mixture come together until all the ingredients are fully mixed up. Simply pour the mixture over ice or into a glass for an instant boost of energy!

Amazing Nutribullet Recipe 14: Life Boost Blaster

1 Tablespoon of organic pumpkin seeds
1 Tablespoon of organic sunflower seeds
1 Organic small apple, without seeds and sliced into quarters
1 Small organic carrot
1 Small ripe banana
1 Cup of fresh organic blueberries
1 Cup of fresh organic baby spinach and kale spinach)
4-5 Pieces of organic asparagus if possible
1 Cup of fresh organic raspberries
1 Tablespoon of flax meal
1 Cup of vanilla soy milk
1 Cup of organic coconut water

The Nutribullet recipe for the Life Boost Blaster is one that I have been using for several months now. My whole family really enjoys it since I have bought the Nutribullet blender. You can make this healthy and delicious this super food cocktail in any regular blender. Unlike the Nutribullet, in this case you might have some small bits and pieces in your drink because other blender are not comparable to the power of the Nutribullet.

I make this or a similar breakfast drink every morning for my family and myself before I get started with my daily work.

If I do not have much time, I prepare this breakfast drink the night before I go to bed.

Just make sure to put all the ingredients in your blender cup and cover it so that the preparation is already done. The next morning I just need to blend the mixture to make a fresh quality drink that tastes like it just has been prepared.

If you do it like this the taste is surprisingly luscious and delicious. It is an extremely delightful and addicting morning breakfast drink.

If you have an allergy and do not support grains, lactose or soy beans, make sure to replace these ingredients with a supplementary portion of veggies or fruits to make it extra fruity and veggie!

This Nutribullet super food breakfast morning cocktail enables a perfect digestion. It includes a variety of veggies, fruits and grains that are particulary important in the morning and with this super drink you will receive a super serving of minerals, vitamins and omega 3 fats.

Ingredients

- ½ tablespoon of organic pumpkin seeds
- ½ tablespoon of organic sunflower seeds
- 1 organic small apple, without seeds and sliced into quarters
- 1 small organic carrot
- 1 small ripe banana
- ½ cup of fresh organic blueberries
- 1 cup of fresh organic baby spinach and kale also called super greens (available in some supermarkets if not replace it with baby spinach)
- 4-5 pieces of organic asparagus if possible
- ½ cup of fresh organic raspberries
- 1 tablespoon of flax meal
- ⅓ cup of vanilla soy milk
- ⅓ cup of organic coconut water

Variation for vegetarians:
- ⅓ cup of organic vanilla yogurt or tofu (this adds more protein)

5 Minute Quick Nutribullet Preparation:

Mill all the seeds first or have them already milled for you. Next add all above ingredients into your blender and mix until everything has a smooth texture.

Amazing Nutribullet Recipe 15: Free Radical Fighter

The Fee Radical Fighter acts as an antioxidant bomb that helps neutralize free radicals in our body and brain.

Antioxidants bind free radicals and they are neutralizing them so that they can not cause any harm to our system.

Antioxidants also help fight against cancerous invaders.

This is an antioxidant free radical killer Nutribullet recipe because it includes some of the top antioxidant ingredients like oranges, spinach, avocado and blueberries.

By the way you can also add some nuts to your liking and if you are consuming just one single Brazil nut you are satisfying your daily supply of the cancer fighting mineral selenium.

Ingredients:

- 1 organic avocado
- 2 handfuls of organic swiss chard
- 1 cup of black berries (organic if possible)
- 1 cup watermelon
- 1/2 of organic blueberries
- 1 organic fig
- 1/2 of organic blueberries
- 1/8 cup of flax seeds (organic if possible)
- Fresh spring water

5 Minute Quick Nutribullet Preparation:

Blend all the ingredients above and the fresh spring water in a Nutribullet blender in the given order and serve as an antioxidant booster in the morning for the best free radical fighting effect!

Amazing Nutribullet Recipe 16: Toxin Cleansing Blast

The Toxin Cleansing Blast is one of my all times favorites. It is a simple but yet effective drink that benefits your body by cleansing it, energizing it and regulating your hormones.

Ingredients:
    1-2 spinach leaves (organic if possible)
    1 pear (organic if possible)
    1 banana (organic if possible)
    1 apple (organic if possible)
    some pineapple juice

5 Minute Quick Nutribullet Preparation:

With the help of a Nutribullet blender simply add the spinach, pear, banana, apple and pineapple juice into the machine.

Turn it on and watch as the fruits and veggies are broken down and pureed.

This smooth tasty treat can be poured into your favorite glass or placed in the fridge for later use.

Amazing Nutribullet Recipe 17: Healthy Yummie Ricotta Dinner

1 Package of frozen spinach

1 Cup of organic non fat Italian ricotta cheese

1 Fresh organic egg

1/4 Cup of shredded mozzarella

4 Lasagna noodles

2 Cups really good self made pasta sauce

Turkey, chicken or other type of meat

A dash of pink Himalaya salt

If you need to quickly improvise and come up with a quick, healthy and delicious dinner idea, I highly recommend to try out your Nutribullet with this amazing non-fat Italian Ricotta recipe.

You can improvise and try the recipe with all kinds of noodles like lasagna noodles or stuffed shells that you can already buy ready to be used in the supermarket.

I like to make this recipe if I am very busy and do not have much time for cooking and my family wishes that I would make this amazing Nutribullet recipe more often.

My kids and husband tell me that this is the yummiest lasagna dish that they have ever had.

Ingredients:

1 package of frozen spinach (organic is best and cooked & rung out)

1 cup of organic non fat Italian ricotta cheese

1 fresh organic egg

1/4 cup of shredded mozzarella (organic if possible and from the buffalo)

4 lasagna noodles (bought in a package and ready to be used)

2 cups really good self made pasta sauce (if you are making the Spaghetti Sauce Recipe that comes with this book then you can use the leftover sauce that you made with the Nutribullet because this is the best sauce you can make and I always make more in order to have some leftover sauce for this recipe)

If you like some left over turkey, chicken or other type of meat

A dash of pink Himalaya salt to your taste

10 Minute Quick Nutribullet Preparation - Baking time: 40 minutes:

Add the first four ingredients into your Nutribullet

Add about 1/3 cups of fresh source water.

Cook the lasagna noodles al dente and put 2 of them on the bottom of a large loaf pan and line it with 1 cut of your Nutribullet pasta sauce. Follow with the blended ingredients from your Nutribullet and followed by the chicken, turkey or other meat, followed by 2 cooked lasagna noodles and finish with one more cup of your Nutribullet pasta sauce. Finishing touch is some pink Himalaya salt.

Bake the Ricotta Lasagna at 350* for 40 minutes. You can do some other tasks while the dish is baking inside your oven so the actual time that you spend in the kitchen is only for the quick preparation time.

Surprise Bonus: The 5 Minute Smoothie Ritual

Let's talk a little bit about how you can do this even if you are a very busy person and still want to get all the healthy and powerful benefits from these smoothies.

I have been consuming these healthy smoothie recipes for three years now, but I only have added Yoga to my lifestyle recently. My sister Alecandra has encouraged me to get started with a Yoga lifestyle and I am very happy I did because something very powerful happened.

Adding a workout like Yoga makes these healthy ingredients that are included in these smoothies so much more powerful and beneficial for your mind and body.

Alecandra was also the one that inspired me to create this book and do it in a way that makes it valuable for someone who already loves to live a healthy lifestyle and in terms of the specific health benefits that come with each ingredient so that a consumer does understand why consuming these smoothies on a daily basis is such a beneficial thing to do.

Once you understand this powerful principle of adding a light workout to your lifestyle, let's now talk about the time aspect which might be a very important thing to you if you are a very busy person.

I have always loved to simplify things (I kind of am a usability nut!) and like to make procedures effortless and 5 minute quick in terms of instructions and usability. My usability tip is to use this book next to your kitchen table as you go through the preparation of your smoothie.

If you like quick to apply and easy to use systems because of your personality or your time constraints, I hope you like the format of this picture book and my usability tips how to consume it in a quick and easy way. I also hope you like the way that I am simplifying the process for you while you are getting the most benefits out of it.

Using this book pretty much like a traditional cookbook makes your daily healthy smoothie consumption process a 5 minute quick, easy and enjoyable process.

Using modern, mobile, interactive and time saving technology is really how you are enabled to make this ritual work for you if you are a very busy person. Use this book like you would use a real cookbook (this "cookbook" technique really makes this beneficial healthy smoothie consumption lifestyle possible for you!)

Alecandra also taught me all of these cool 5 minute time management and usability techniques that she likes to include in her own meditation and yoga ritual to make it work for her. Integrating usability and time management tips into your own smoothie consumption ritual is exactly how you enable and empower yourself to transform your life into a healthy smoothie lifestyle!

You can learn more about Alecandra's cool ways of integrating usability and time management into a daily lifestyle and this is especially valuable for you if you are applying a daily workout like yoga and or meditation. She will show you some cool time and usability tricks and without any effort and in 5 minutes flat! She really knows how to integrate these beneficial disciplines into one's daily lifestyle.

Nutribullet Quiz

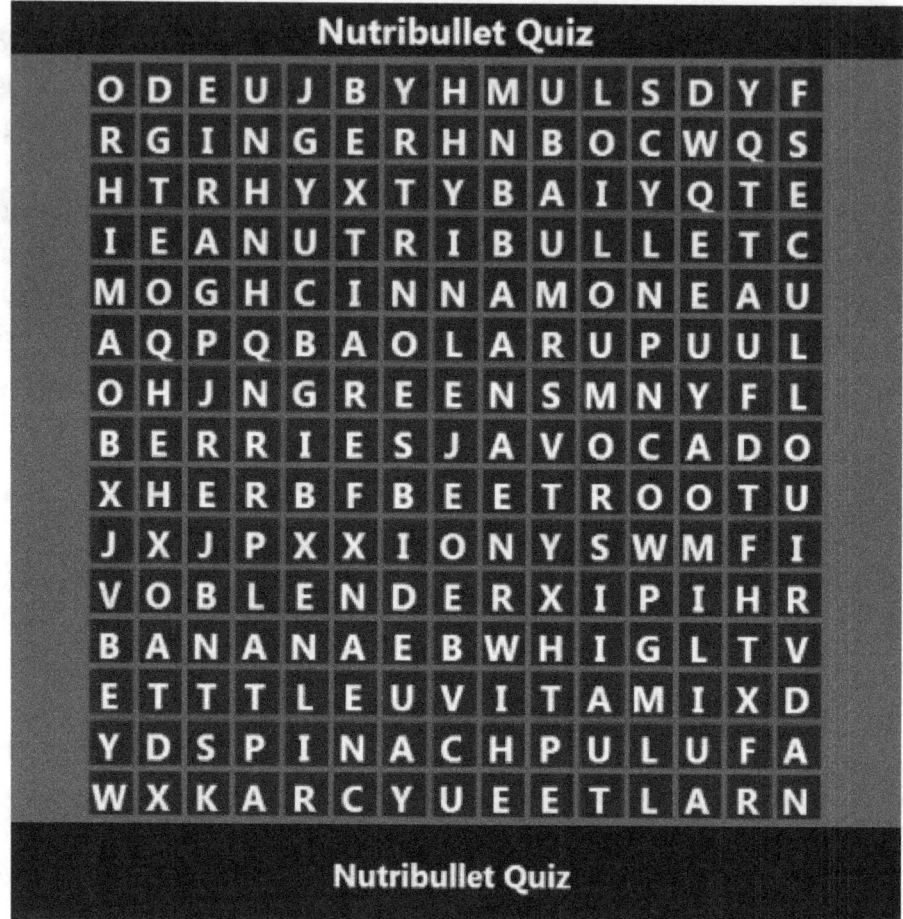

All you have to do is find 12 clean eating and clean drinking high-speed blender Ingredient related words. Use your imagination, read backwards, sideways, and forwards to find the correct words and associations. Go to the next page to see the correct answers!

Have fun:)

Quiz Answers

1. Nutribullet
2. Vitamix
3. Greens
4. Spinach
5. Blender
6. Berries
7. Banana
8. Ginger
9. Herb
10. Cinnamon
11. Beetroot
12. Avocado

Conclusion

My goal with these high-speed recipes (in my case Nutribullet recipes) is to give you some clean eating and clean drinking 5 minute quick to make delicious & healthy recipe options.

If you drink and eat these healthy and nutritious 5 minute quick clean drink and clean food recipes on a daily basis and add a daily workout plan like yoga or any other workout to your daily chores, you will take even more benefits out of these recipes.

I love these recipes as they help me keep healthy, lean as well as satisfied.

Each day I will use one or more of these wonderful recipes as a meal replacement for breakfast, lunch or dinner. The best part about using these different drinks is they actually work!

You will definitely feel better after having these recipes as the ingredients come together to balance and regulate the hormones of your body.

Also, all of the ingredients that you need to make these recipes can be found at your local market for less than $9 which makes them affordable on top of it.

I hope I have delivered and fulfilled my promises and I hope that you are taking action on your own healthy lifestyle goals. If you do, you are going to be hooked for life!

I encourage you to take note of the many benefits that come with each different clean & healthy food and drink ingredient that comes with each different recipe.

I also encourage you to take the book/device with you as you go and prepare each individual recipe.

Just keep the book on your mobile device next to your working table and go through one recipe at a time and as you progress. The book is intended to be used as a mental stimulation and to motivate you to take action at the same time.

I tried to make it as effortless, entertaining, inspirational and easy to use and consume as possible.

I hope you will use and consume the content whenever you need some quick and easy, healthy and delicious clean eating and drink high-speed blender recipe instructions. If you really use it as it is intended to be used (use it as you go through the recipes and keep the book close during your preparation time!) it is a very powerful way of discovering the unlimited world of clean eat and drink high-speed blender recipes!

Remember, all you have to do is open the book and start with the first recipe preparation that you like to get started with. Go through all of them and apply them on a daily basis as you see fit and depending on the health benefits that you are looking to achieve.

You just need a bit of time (5 minutes per preparation is enough only 2 of the dinner recipes need a little bit more prep time and cooking and baking time) to be able to make at least one high-speed blender (Nutribullet) recipe per day. You can repeat the 5 minute quick preparation time as you see fit during your day.

For example, I am really big on Smoothies because they have helped me beat my Asthma in combination with a daily Yoga workout and therefore I am consuming at least 3 high-speed smoothies during the day when I am at home and it takes me not more than 15 minutes per day with the help of my beloved Nutribullet blender.

Everyone has a different goal, but these 5 minute quick and easy recipes that I have been able to perfect with the Nutribullet have certainly made my life easier.

Remember, you can achieve the maximum of health benefits from consuming these healthy high-speed blender (Nutribullet) recipes, too. You do not have to focus on Smoothies like me, but replacing the unhealthy food options with these types of healthy ingredients rich recipes is the first step to a healthier and easier to manage lifestyle. In combination with a light workout these recipes really do wonderful things for your body and brain!

Once you have achieved your own goal that you are looking to achieve with these amazing high-speed blender (Nutribullet) recipes by following these easy to follow instructions, you can go ahead and discover even more of these healthy and clean food and drink ingredients and what they can do for you.

I believe with all the above high-speed blender (Nutribullet) recipes, you will become a healthy and energized person making you more productive in your day to day activities.

I am already working on some more clean food and drink high-speed blender recipes for you and once I am done proving and testing them, I will release them as Volume 2 of this series.

Did you love *Smoothie Recipe Book To Gain Energy & Detox 17 Smoothie Bowl Recipes, Cleanse Drinks & Blender Mix Recipes To Feel Stronger*? Then you should read *Fasting Book For Health, Fitness, Weight Loss & Detoxing 11 Juicing For Beginners Recipes With delicious & Healthy Fruit & Vegetable Juices* by Juliana Baltimoore!

Fasting Book For Health, Fitness, Weight Loss & Detoxing 11 Juicing For Beginners Recipes With delicious & Healthy Fruit & Vegetable Juices...Using a combination of these delicious healthy low calorie juicing recipes from this collection plus following a strict 2 month Juicing diet with the juicing recipes that are included in this book, the author has been able to lose 40 lbs over two months. She has been able to stick to healthy juices after her juicing diet and this change of habit has helped her develop and maintain a lean body and a clear mind. Inside you will learn what juicing can do for you. There is an unlimited array of health benefits of juicing and Juicing to loose weight is one aspect of juicing. Inside this book Juliana will focus on juicing to loose weight and show you exactly how she lost 40 lbs in 60 days, but here are some more powerful benefits that you might consider about the power of getting yourself into a juicing habit: Applying a daily juicing ritual will not only make your body lean, it will also provide your body with unlimited health benefits. These are just some of the health benefits that come with a daily juicing ritual. There is truly an unlimited amount of health benefits that comes with juicing. Here are the most important ones: Weight Loss Antioxidants Alzheimer's Prevention Asthma Help (I suffered for years from breathing problems and Asthma and finally was able to get rid of it because of my daily Juicing and Smoothie ritual) Blood Cleanse Arthritis Prevention Bone Protection Cancer Prevention Cervical Cancer Prevention Breast Cancer Prevention Colon Cancer Prevention Liver Cancer Prevention Lung Cancer Prevention Prostate Cancer Prevention Cataracts Prevention Ovarian Cancer Prevention Stomach Cancer Prevention Digestion Detoxification Energy Digestion Heart Disease Prevention Immune System Hydration Improving Eyesight Improved Complexion Increased Blood Circulation Kidney Cleanse Increased Libido Liver Cleanse Lower Blood Pressure Lower Cholesterol Macular Degeneration Prevention Mental Health Osteoporosis Prevention Pain Relief Reduce Inflammation Reduce Water Retention Stroke Prevention and an unlimited amount of other health benefits. Juicing is a simple to acquire skill and if you turn this skill into a habit, you will be able to live a health, fit, clean, toxin free and lean life from the inside out and for a very long time. Juicing keeps the doctor away and doubles your life! See you inside where you will discover the power of juicing to loose weight. Follow these amazing juicing vegetables, juicing fruits, juicing alkaline, juicing raw & juicing paleo juicing to loose weight recipes, 5 minute quick to make and delicious fat burning juices & weight loss blender juice recipes today and keep the doctor away...this juicing ritual will double your happiness and health so get started today...

About the Publisher

InfinitYou is a hybrid general interest trade publisher. One of the first of its kind InfinitYou publishes physical books, electronic books, and audiobooks in various genres. Our publications are meant to educate, edify and entertain readers of all walks of life from babies to the elderly. Home to more than twenty imprints such as Infinit Baby, Infinit Kids, Infinit Girl, Infinit Boy, Infinit Coloring, Infinit Swear Words, Infinit Activities, Infinit Productivity, Infinit Cat, Infinit Dog, Infinit Love, Infinit Family, Infinit Survival, Infinit Health, Infinit Beauty, Infinit Spirituality, Infinit Lifestyle, Infinit Wealth, Infinit Romance, and lots more.

www.ingramcontent.com/pod-product-compliance
Lightning Source LLC
LaVergne TN
LVHW020435080526
838202LV00055B/5200